ghosts don't have bodies

by

evy klassen

illustrated by

ME kingcott

I am inspired by people like my great-nephew Levi.
He is always up to the challenge of celebrating life in his body.

To Michele, who spoke out the idea to write this book.

evy

To my husband Greg, for your endless support
and delight in my art journey.

In honour of my father, LE Edwards,
who suggested I could write a book.

Surprise! I illustrated one instead!

ME kingcott

For

From

Ghosts
don't have bodies,
but guess what?

I do!

I have a body that can dance

and arms that swing,

a tongue that's for licking,
lips that kiss and sing.

My legs, knees, and feet

places.

high

to

me

take

My eyes see beauty in nature,

words,

and faces.

I have fingers made for touching

and ears that like to hear.

My back leads to my butt
which sticks out from my rear!

My teeth and my mouth munch up
food really fast.

My mind remembers songs
and funny stories from the past.

Sometimes I get sick,
and my body feels so weak.

My nose gets all snotty,

and my throat hurts to speak.

I sneeze and I wheeze

and I cough like a seal.

BUT

my body is a fighter
and finds lots of ways to heal.

Sometimes I say mean things

about my body or my hair.

I look around at others,
find it hard to not compare.

I wonder what my body
wants to say to me.

Could I learn to listen

and treat myself respectfully?

If all that I have said
about my body is true,

then if you have a body,
it might be true for you too!

Some of us can talk a lot!

Some can't say what's in their heads.

Some of us move so fast

some have to stay in bed.

I might dress to show my style,

to suit the weather or my mood,

but when you and I were born
we were both completely nude!

How should we celebrate
the colours and shades of skin we wear,

our different shapes of bodies,
our different types of hair?

Our bodies are the homes

that house you and me,

releasing us yet keeping us
from being completely free.

Without them

I guess

we would

just

be

ghosts.

Ghosts don't have bodies
to eat jam and toast.

Ghosts don't have bodies as you and I do.

It's because of our bodies
that I can know **YOU!**

 FriesenPress

One Printers Way
Altona, MB R0G 0B0
Canada

www.friesenpress.com

ISBN
978-1-03-916415-4 (Hardcover)
978-1-03-916414-7 (Paperback)
978-1-03-916416-1 (eBook)

1. JUVENILE NONFICTION, SOCIAL TOPICS, SELF-ESTEEM & SELF-RELIANCE

Distributed to the trade by The Ingram Book Company

CPSIA information can be obtained
at www.ICGtesting.com
Printed in the USA
LVHW081032100423
743733LV00001B/2

9 781039 164147